UNLESS 7 LORD BUILDS THE HOUSE

— A Devotional on Marriage —

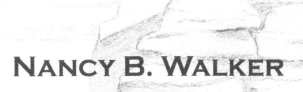

NANCY B. WALKER

ILLUSTRATED BY SAMANTHA WALKER

MW00899613

Paraphrases are the author's based on the NIV translation.
All scripture quotations were taken from THE HOLY BIBLE, NEW INTERNATIONAL VERSION®, NIV® Copyright © 1973, 1978, 1984, 2011 by Biblica, Inc.® Used by permission. All rights reserved worldwide.

WestBow Press books may be ordered through booksellers or by contacting:

WestBow Press
A Division of Thomas Nelson & Zondervan
1663 Liberty Drive
Bloomington, IN 47403
www.westbowpress.com
1 (866) 928-1240

ISBN: 978-1-5127-6553-3 (sc)
ISBN: 978-1-5127-6552-6 (e)

Library of Congress Control Number: 2016920742

Print information available on the last page.

WestBow Press rev. date: 01/27/2017

WESTBOW
PRESS®
A DIVISION OF THOMAS NELSON
& ZONDERVAN

DEDICATION

To my wonderful son, Craig, and his sweet wife, Samantha.
Your level of devotion to the LORD and desire to serve
Him in all aspects of your lives continually amazes me.

INTRODUCTION

I originally wrote this devotional for my niece, Jill, to be given at her bridal luncheon. While she and her fiancé were already strong Christians, I wanted to compile scriptures that would remind her of God's plan for marriage.

My inspiration came from Psalm 127:1, "Unless the LORD builds the house, you labor in vain." My thought was to give Jill principles from God's word that she could refer back to and upon which she could build a Biblical marriage and thus a happy home.

As I started pulling together scriptures to use, I found several of them to have a strong visual component that tied into the concept of building a home. I imagined a house built on a rock, with an exposed foundation, that had columns holding up the roof. Since my niece had eight bride's maids, I needed ten house parts that would have scripture verses associated with them — one for the mother of the bride, the mother of the groom and one for each of the bride's maids. So, in addition to the rock, the foundation, and six columns, I decided to also use the front door and the roof.

I explained my concept to my daughter-in-law, Samantha, and asked her to draw a house like the one I had imagined. She captured it perfectly.

Before framing the drawing of the house as a gift for Jill, I wrote each principle directly onto it, on the corresponding house part. I then made a color copy which I cut up by principle, and therefore by house part. My thought was that at the luncheon, as we read about each principle, we could put the house parts together and "build" the house.

I made copies of each of the scriptures and gave one to each of the mothers of the bride and groom and to each of the bride's maids. After each scripture was read, I attached that part of the house to the others. Then I would read the commentary on the importance of that principle. At the end, we had a memorable visual of God's plan for marriage.

My niece and several of the other ladies at the luncheon were so moved by what I had put together that I thought other couples might be blessed by hearing this too. My prayer is that all who hear or read this devotional will be reminded of the importance of building our homes and our lives on God's principles.

THE OPENING

Marriage is one of the most complicated but grandest adventures that the Lord puts before us. Until you are married, it is hard to understand just how challenging it can be to merge two lives, two ways of approaching a problem, two styles of communicating and two sets of differing priorities.

The good news is that there is a comprehensive marriage manual that addresses every joy, sorrow, triumph and heartbreak your marriage will face. It is the Bible. In it, the LORD gives you the blueprint for creating a marriage that will thrive in every situation that you will face, good or bad.

Even with God's word to guide you, building and maintaining a strong marriage is hard work; but it sure can be fun, and definitely is an adventure.

Then the LORD God said, "It is not good that the man should be alone; I will make him a helper fit for him." [1]

"Then the LORD God made a woman from the rib he had taken out of the man, and he brought her to the man. The man said, 'This is now bone of my bones and flesh of my flesh …' For this reason a man will leave his father and mother and be united to his wife, and they will become one flesh." [2]

BUT: *"Unless the LORD builds the house, its builders labor in vain."* [3]

THE ROCK

"Everyone then who hears these words of mine and does them will be like a wise man who built his house on the rock. And the rain fell, and the floods came, and the winds blew and beat on that house, but it did not fall, because it had been founded on the rock."
Matthew 7:24-25

IF YOU ARE IN A RELATIONSHIP WITH JESUS CHRIST, THEN EACH OF YOU IS ALREADY STANDING ON THE ROCK - THE ROCK OF YOUR SALVATION. NOW AS YOU JOIN YOUR LIVES TOGETHER, BUILD YOUR HOME ON THIS SAME ROCK.

JESUS CHRIST IS THIS ROCK. FOLLOWING HIS PRECEPTS IS THE ONLY SURE WAY YOUR MARRIAGE WILL HAVE STABILITY, SECURITY, LOVE, AND TRUST THAT WILL ENDURE FOR A LIFETIME.

THERE IS NO ROCK LIKE OUR GOD.[1]

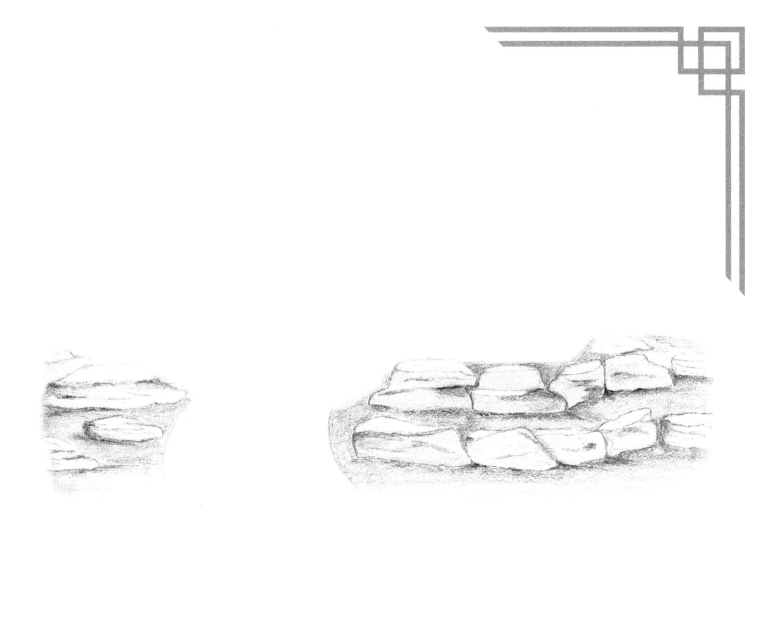

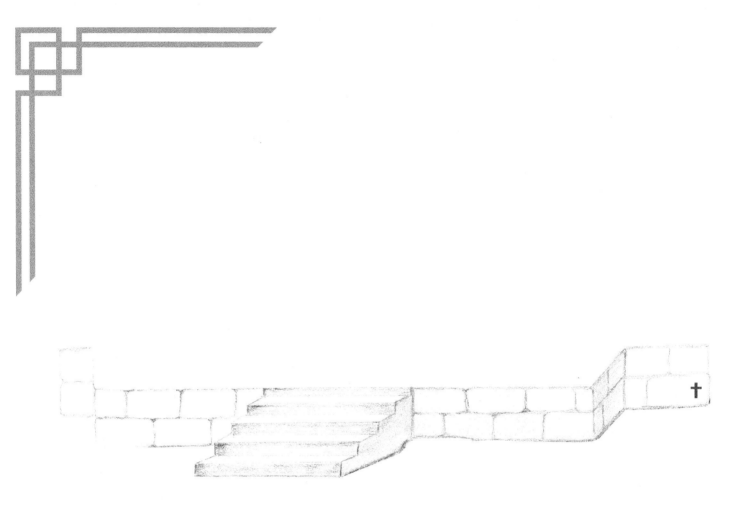

A SURE FOUNDATION

"So this is what the Sovereign LORD says: 'See, I lay a stone in Zion, a tested stone, a precious cornerstone for a sure foundation; the one who trusts will never be dismayed.'" Isaiah 28:16

THE CORNERSTONE IS THE FIRST STONE PLACED WHEN CONSTRUCTING A BRICK OR STONE FOUNDATION. IT'S PLACEMENT IS IMPORTANT BECAUSE ALL THE OTHER STONES WILL BE SET IN REFERENCE TO THIS STONE, THUS DETERMINING THE POSITION AND STABILITY OF THE ENTIRE STRUCTURE. THE FOUNDATION IS WHAT EVERYTHING ELSE RESTS ON. ANY MISTAKES MADE IN THE FOUNDATION WILL EXPONENTIALLY IMPACT YOUR ENTIRE HOME.

WHEN YOU CHOOSE JESUS CHRIST AS YOUR CORNERSTONE, YOUR HOME WILL HAVE A SOLID FOUNDATION ABLE TO SUPPORT THE WEIGHT OF ALL OF LIFE'S TROUBLES AND ABLE TO WEATHER ANY STORM.

PILLAR OF FAITH

*"Now faith is being sure of what we hope for
and certain of what we do not see."*
Hebrews 11:1

FAITH IS ONLY AS POWERFUL AS THE OBJECT OF YOUR FAITH. THE WORLD SAYS "JUST HAVE FAITH;" BUT FAITH IN WHAT?

THE OBJECT OF YOUR FAITH MUST BE JESUS CHRIST. FAITH IN HIM, AND THEREFORE HIS WORD, IS ESSENTIAL FOR A STRONG MARRIAGE. ONLY HE PROVIDES THE TOOLS AND THE BLUEPRINT FOR AN ABUNDANT LIFE TOGETHER.

Faith

Wisdom

PILLAR OF WISDOM

*"By wisdom a house is built, and through understanding
it is established; through knowledge its rooms are
filled with rare and beautiful treasures."*
Proverbs 24:3-2

Of course that verse is talking about God's wisdom not the world's wisdom. While sometimes God's wisdom seems counter intuitive, we know that man's "wisdom" is not always wise.

As the creator of all things, including man, only God truly knows how everything works best. He shares His wisdom with you through His word. If you know and apply His wisdom to your marriage, it will be joyous and strong.

PILLAR OF COMMITTMENT

"Some Pharisees came and tested [Jesus] by asking,
"Is it lawful for a man to divorce his wife?"
...at the beginning of creation God 'made them male and female. For
this reason a man will leave his father and mother and be united to
his wife, and the two will become one flesh.' So they are no longer two,
but one. Therefore what God has joined together, let man not separate."
Mark 10:2, 6-9

MARRIAGE IS NOT JUST AN AGREEMENT OR A CONTRACT. IT IS A COVENANT RELATIONSHIP INSTITUTED BY GOD; A *SOLEMN VOW* BEFORE GOD, BINDING TWO PEOPLE TOGETHER PERMANENTLY.

TO ENTER THE SACRED COVENANT OF MARRIAGE MEANS TO BE WILLING TO MAKE A *TOTAL, EXCLUSIVE COMMITMENT* TO YOUR MARRIAGE PARTNER, THUS THE VOWS — "FOR BETTER AND FOR WORSE, FOR RICHER AND FOR POORER, IN SICKNESS AND IN HEALTH."

BUT THE MARVELOUS THING ABOUT A MARRIAGE OF COMPLETE COMMITMENT IS THAT IT IS A RELATIONSHIP OF UNCONDITIONAL LOVE AND GRACE. THIS GIVES YOU ACCEPTANCE, SECURITY, AND A PARTNER WITH WHOM YOU CAN FACE THE TRIALS AND SHARE THE JOYS OF THIS LIFE.

Committment

Respect

PILLAR OF RESPECT

"Honor one another above yourselves."
Romans 12:10b

TO THE BRIDE

IN EPHESIANS 5 AND 1 PETER 3, WHERE GOD SPEAKS OF THE MARRIAGE RELATIONSHIP, HE NEVER INSTRUCTS THE WIFE TO LOVE HER HUSBAND. RATHER, HE SAYS THAT SHE MUST RESPECT HIM. WHY IS THAT? HE CREATED MAN, SO HE KNOWS WHAT A MAN NEEDS MOST FROM HIS WIFE — RESPECT. TO FEEL LOVED BY HIS WIFE, A HUSBAND MUST FEEL HER RESPECT.

TO THE GROOM

WHILE FEELING LOVED IS MOST ESSENTIAL TO YOUR BRIDE, YOUR RESPECT FOR HER IS IMPORTANT TO A HAPPY MARRIAGE. IF YOU DO NOT RESPECT HER, YOU WILL NOT LOVE HER; AND IF YOU DO NOT TREAT HER WITH RESPECT, SHE WILL NOT RESPECT YOU.

PILLAR OF SUBMISSION

"Submit to one another out of reverence for Christ."
Ephesians 5:21

THAT VERSE IS OFTEN OVERLOOKED IN THE RUSH TO GET TO THE NEXT VERSES THAT SAY: "WIVES, SUBMIT TO YOUR HUSBANDS AS TO THE LORD. FOR THE HUSBAND IS THE HEAD OF THE WIFE AS CHRIST IS THE HEAD OF THE CHURCH ..."[1]

EVERY INSTITUTION NEEDS STRUCTURE TO FUNCTION AS IT WAS INTENDED. GOD INTENDED THE INSTITUTION OF MARRIAGE TO HAVE ONE HEAD, JUST AS THE CHURCH HAS ONE HEAD, CHRIST. HAVING TWO HEADS CAN LEAD TO CONFLICT, DISUNITY, UNCERTAINTY, AND DEGRADATION OF TRUST.

IN GEN 2:18, GOD RECOGNIZED THE MAN'S NEED FOR A HELPER, NOT A DOORMAT. A HELPER SPEAKS UP, ASKS QUESTIONS THAT LEAD TO UNDERSTANDING, AND PROVIDES INFORMATION THAT LEADS TO A RESOLUTION. BUT A HELPER HELPS, NOT LEADS; AND A LEADER LEADS, NOT DICTATES

Submission

Intimacy

PILLAR OF INTIMACY

"For this reason a man will leave his father and mother and
be united to his wife, and they will become one flesh."
Genesis 2:24

THE "ONE FLESH" IN THAT VERSE IS USUALLY CONSIDERED TO BE PHYSICAL INTIMACY; BUT IT ALSO REFERS TO EMOTIONAL AND SPIRITUAL INTIMACY. WHILE MEN TEND TO SEEK PHYSICAL INTIMACY, WOMEN TEND TO SEEK EMOTIONAL INTIMACY. OFTEN NEITHER SEEKS SPIRITUAL INTIMACY.

SPIRITUAL INTIMACY CAN BE ACHIEVED BY READING GOD'S WORD TOGETHER, WORSHIPING TOGETHER, BUT ESPECIALLY BY PRAYING WITH AND FOR EACH OTHER. WITHOUT SPIRITUAL INTIMACY, YOUR PHYSICAL AND EMOTIONAL INTIMACY WILL NOT BE AS RICH AS THEY CAN BE. THE LORD MUST BE BROUGHT INTO THE MARRIAGE IN ALL THREE AREAS AND NONE OF THE THREE SHOULD BE NEGLECTED.

THE DOOR

"A wife of noble character who can find?"
"She is clothed with strength and dignity; she can laugh
at the days to come. She speaks with wisdom, and faithful
instruction is on her tongue. She watches over the affairs of
her household and does not eat the bread of idleness."
Proverbs 31:10, 25-27

THE WIFE HAS A GREAT AMOUNT OF CONTROL OVER WHAT COMES INTO AND WHAT GOES ON INSIDE YOUR HOME. HUSBANDS ARE LIKE THERMOMETERS; THEY READ THE TEMPERATURE IN THE HOUSE AND ACT ACCORDINGLY. THE WIFE IS THE THERMOSTAT; SHE CONTROLS THE TEMPERATURE. AS THE SAYING GOES, "IF MAMA AIN'T HAPPY; AIN'T NOBODY HAPPY."

AS A PROVERBS 31 WIFE, YOU CAN MAKE THE TEMPERATURE INSIDE YOUR HOME ONE OF JOY AND PEACE.

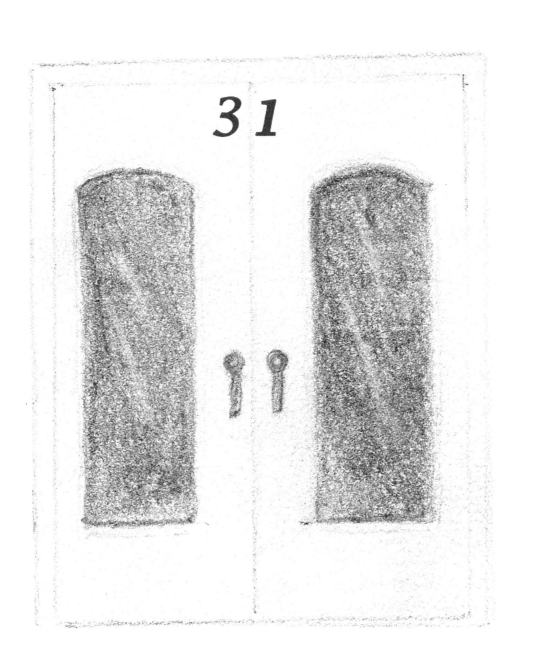

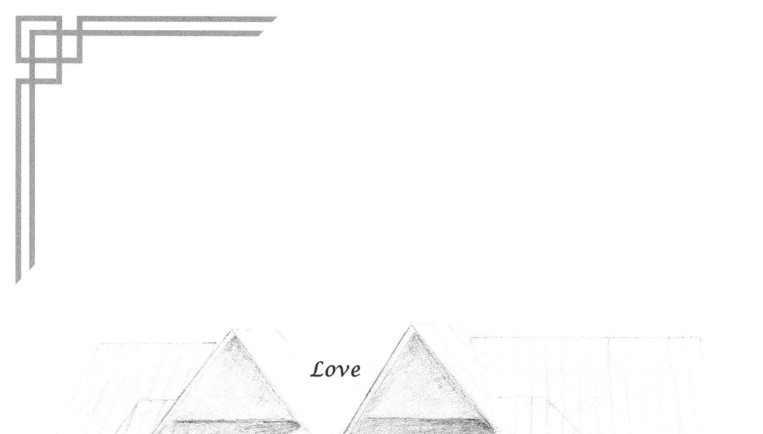

Love

COVERED WITH LOVE

Above all, love each other deeply, because love
covers over a multitude of sins."
1 Peter 4:8

THE GREEK WORD FOR LOVE IN THIS VERSE IS *AGAPE*. IT IS A LOVE OF CHOICE, NOT JUST OF EMOTION OR FRIENDSHIP. IT IS DESCRIBED IN 1 CORINTHIANS 13 AS BEING PATIENT AND KIND, NOT ENVIOUS, BOASTFUL OR PROUD. IT IS NOT RUDE, SELFISH, OR EASILY ANGERED. IT DOES NOT KEEP A RECORD OF WRONGS AND DOES NOT ENJOY EVIL, BUT REJOICES IN TRUTH. IT ALWAYS PROTECTS, ALWAYS TRUSTS, ALWAYS HOPES, AND ALWAYS PERSEVERES.[1]

THIS IS THE LOVE THAT GOD INTENDED A HUSBAND AND WIFE TO SHARE, WHICH CAN ONLY BE EXPERIENCED IN A MARRIAGE THAT IS CHRIST-CENTERED. A MARRIAGE COVERED IN LOVE PROVIDES A SHELTER FROM ALL OF LIFE'S TRIALS AND A PLATFORM FOR ALL OF LIFE'S JOYS. IT ALLOWS YOU TO BE VULNERABLE AND COMPLETELY OPEN WITH YOUR SPOUSE, KNOWING THAT YOU WILL ALWAYS BE SAFE PHYSICALLY, EMOTIONALLY AND SPIRITUALLY.

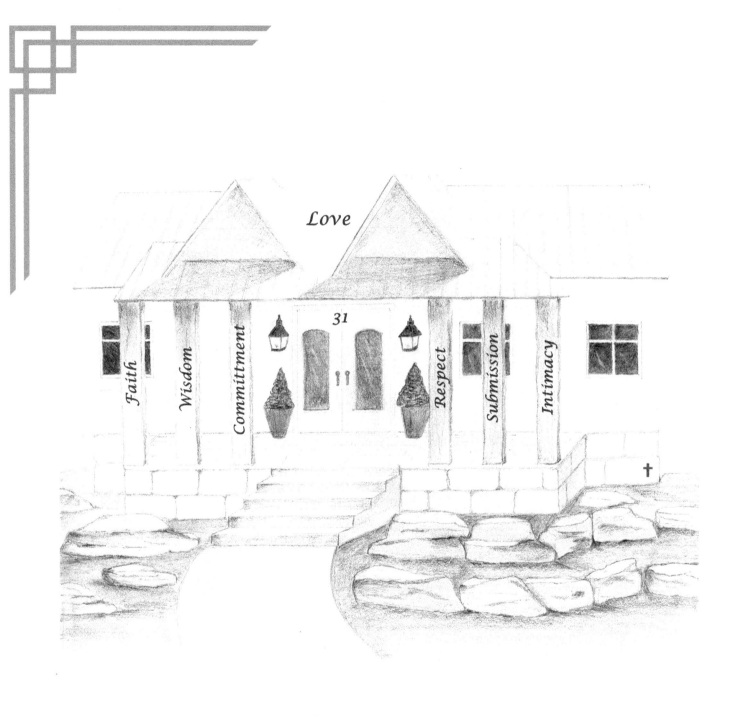

IN CLOSING

Proverbs 14:1 says: "The wise woman <u>builds</u> her house ..."

Building a house takes deliberate action; it doesn't build itself. A strong marriage is the same. It takes time, focus and hard work. But most importantly, it takes using the right component parts.

With Christ as your cornerstone, and God's word as your guide, your home and your marriage will be filled with unwavering faith, Godly wisdom, complete commitment, mutual respect, appropriate submission, and true intimacy. Your marriage will thrive in an atmosphere of joy, peace and love.

Marriage may be hard work, but it definitely is a grand adventure!

On the following page is the image of the house that you can cut out, if you wish, to "build" the house at your marriage event.

END NOTES

THE OPENING

[1] Genesis 2:18

[2] Genesis 2:22- 23a, 24

[3] Psalm 127:1

THE ROCK

[1] 1 Sam 2:2

PILLAR OF SUBMISSION

[1] Ephesians 5:22-23a

COVERED WITH LOVE

[1] 1 Corinthians 13:4-7

ACKNOWLEDGEMENTS

First I want to thank my husband, Jim, who supports me in everything that I do and lovingly puts up with my tendency to put my foot in my mouth.

Thank you to my wonderful daughter-in-law, Samantha, who agreed to draw the illustrations. I loved the time we spent together working on this book.

Many thanks to my friend, Jo Boggs, who walked with me through this process, continually reminding me that everything occurs in the Lord's timing.

Thanks also to Vivien McMahon and Elizabeth Starkey for their enthusiastic encouragement.

But most of all, I thank my Lord and Savior Jesus Christ for calling me to be His.

CPSIA information can be obtained
at www.ICGtesting.com
Printed in the USA
LVOW06s0106070217
523425LV00041B/1122/P